EMOTIONAL EMPOWERMENT: KILLING EMOTIONS

DENNIS E. BRADFORD, Ph.D.

By the Same Author

To

Amy

Contents

1:

Examining Life

Let's begin with a story. Although it's a true anecdote from Allen Broadmann, since *the most interesting topic to you is your own life*, let's make you its protagonist.

Imagine yourself as a member of an organization that has rented a retreat center for a week of training. Not only are you given 3 meals daily, but you have access to its kitchen 24 hours a day in case you'd like coffee, tea, or a snack.

Well before the scheduled breakfast the first morning you toddle bleary-eyed into the kitchen hoping to find some brewed coffee. No luck. You find cans of ground coffee, drip coffee machines, coffee filters for those machines, and measuring spoons – in other words, everything required to brew coffee – but no coffee that was ready to drink.

You notice that another guest is using a kind of funnel on top of a coffee mug, but never having used such a device before and not really wanting to bother brewing coffee, you make cup of tea. You also make a mental note to try that device some other time.

The second morning you also fail to find brewed coffee. So, you attempt using the pour-over device. Except that you use way too much coffee, it works fine.

The third morning you also fail to find brewed coffee. You conclude that the retreat center has no interest in brewing coffee for its guests. You use the pour-over device again.

While waiting for it to finish dripping through, you notice the breakfast cook enter the kitchen, put his mug under what looked like an empty drip-coffee machine, and press a lever. Presto! Freshly brewed coffee filled his mug as its aroma filled the kitchen.

After he exits the kitchen, you examine the machine he used. You've never seen a coffee-making machine like it. It lacks a carafe and dispenses brewed coffee directly into a cup or mug. Interesting.

That's a simple story with four profound implications.

Notice first *how your belief guided your behavior* for three mornings. Even though your belief that there was no freshly brewed coffee was false, your actions were governed by it as if it were true.

Notice second *how your initial ignorance was cured*. You naturally assumed that your belief was true and proceeded accordingly until you happened accidentally to notice that it was false.

You also weren't wearing your glasses. When you did look carefully at the unfamiliar coffee machine after the cook used it, you noticed a small message that someone had thoughtfully taped to it: "Press level down to dispense coffee." So, in fact, the world had offered you all the information you needed to correct your false belief, but you simply missed it.

Notice third *how one false belief easily and naturally spawned another one*, namely, that the retreat center had no interest in brewing coffee for its guests.

Once those false beliefs were in place, they were there indefinitely without your having to do anything to reinforce them. **Once there's a belief, it persists until changed** (or, of course, until death). Whether true or false, beliefs persist indefinitely without our having to sustain them.

Notice fourth that *you had no intention of believing anything false*. It just happened haphazardly due to ordinary circumstances. It wasn't as if you were somehow a defective, evil, or stupid person. You didn't deliberately choose to believe falsely.

So?

Not only do false beliefs arise due to similar ordinary circumstances, but also in the real world many people deliberately try to get us to hold false beliefs. For example, many marketers want you to believe that their product or service is the best even when it isn't. For example, many politicians want your support even if that's not really in your best interest.

Beliefs are just thoughts to which we attach because we judge them to be true. Once we attach to a thought, we simply stay attached indefinitely as long as we fail deliberately to question or challenge it. Furthermore, **one false belief may easily spawn others;** we often layer additional false beliefs on top of an initially false one.

We're all busy. We're all tempted by incessant distractions. If nothing else, healthy brains constantly come up with distracting thoughts.

Obviously, the cure for false beliefs is to attach only to thoughts that withstand serious questioning. Who, though, has time to do that? We should make the time. Why?

Think of the damage caused by false beliefs. For example, some believe that women are naturally inferior to men. Some believe that blacks are naturally inferior to whites. Some believe that non-Chinese are naturally inferior to Chinese. Some believe that non-Christians are inferior to Christians. Some believe that homosexuals are naturally inferior to heterosexuals. Some believe that Jews are inferior to Germans. And so on and on and on.

The damage is compounded when false beliefs lead to other false beliefs. Small ones may lead to large ones. It's not just specific beliefs about which there is disagreement, it's about sets of them, worldviews.

The result is that we live in a world of incessant conflict.

Sometimes the conflict is beneficial when it causes a re-examination of beliefs. This can occur when, for example, a younger generation challenges the beliefs of an older generation.

Often, though, the conflict results in emotional trauma, physical injury, and death. Religious and political wars are commonplace. What's the alternative?

Peace.

How are we able to work towards peace? It's by ceaseless, honest questioning of our own beliefs as well as those of others. Our choice is either to make time to question well or to pay the full cost for not taking the time to question well.

Peace trumps war. Love trumps hate. Unity trumps division.

If you agree, resolve to do your best to be a philosopher. To be a philosopher is to lead an examined life, which is a life of ceaseless, honest questioning with the ultimate goal of living well or wisely.

Are most people philosophers? Of course not. Look at the damage human beings have done to each other, to animals, and to the planet that is our home. It's insane. It's madness. It's dysfunctional.

Will luck or accident cure the insanity? It hasn't yet, and there's no reason to think that it will in the future.

What will cure the insanity?

I suggest **the only kind of cure** that has ever worked in what follows. The point of this opening chapter is to encourage you to value the wisdom of being a philosopher, of leading an examined life. That's not the cure itself, but it is the beginning of the cure. It is the beginning of the way to wisdom.

Do not restrict your questions. *All* beliefs should be questioned. Because beliefs depend upon thoughts, that means that *all* thoughts should be questioned.

Are you willing to do that? If so, you're a philosopher. If not, you're a fanatic. The problem with being a fanatic is that you'll endure unnecessary suffering [misery, distress, agony, anguish, worry] as long as you live. Staying fanatically stuck to a set of static beliefs in a world of incessant flux guarantees that. I first learned about the wisdom of avoiding fanaticism from reading Eric Hoffer's The True Believer many years ago.

There's no middle ground in theory. In practice, you may never succeed in questioning all your beliefs, but, if you are a philosopher, at least you'll be open to questioning all of them and not be fettered by a foolishly restricted inquiry.

The best procedure, as Descartes emphasized, is to question categories of foundational beliefs such as beliefs grounded on perception as well as categories of important beliefs such as beliefs grounded on emotions. I've discussed the former elsewhere [for example, in Mastery in 7 Steps]. Let's here focus on the latter.

Mother Nature gave us emotions in order to predispose us to act appropriately and quickly without needing to think deliberately. Thinking through alternative actions is so slow that it can be deadly.

One time my mother, my wife, and I were standing outside the garages at my parents' lake house. In those days there was an undeveloped gravel pit surrounded by trees on the other side of the road. My mother noticed someone near the edge of the woods on the other side of the road, and he was holding a rifle that was pointed in our direction!

As I looked, ex-soldier that I am, I naturally stepped inside the open garage door to protect myself. I didn't think about taking cover. I just did it. As soon as I realized that my mother and wife were still exposed, I jerked them inside the garage as well.

(My youngest brother and I grabbed a firearm, yelled, and ran after that fellow. We crossed the road and scoured the nearby woods and gravel pit, but he ran away and successfully eluded us. We reported the incident to the police, and, to the best of my understanding, that was the end of it. Maybe he was just using the rifle's scope as a telescope, but maybe not.)

I don't know what you do when someone points a gun at you, but my reaction is to take cover. I don't have to wonder what to do; I just do it. Whether you relate to that example or not, it does demonstrate how emotions work. Fear can prompt fast, prudent action.

Thoughts, beliefs, and actions can all spawn conflict. Let's examine emotions if for no other reason than to try to ensure that we minimize their deleterious effects.

2:

Maximizing Your Experience

Suppose, then, that you'd like to shed false beliefs about emotions, that you'd like to examine your life in terms of emotions. What's the best way to proceed?

The good news is that you're already very experienced emotionally. You've spent decades enduring unwanted emotions and enjoying desired emotions. You're not an unwritten tablet, a blank slate, or an empty page. So, there's no need to start from scratch.

What's the best way to maximize your experience? What's the best way to benefit from all those emotions you've already had? Ideally, it would be by using **the Socratic method**. Socrates was an ancient Greek philosopher who taught people by using skillful questions to enable them to think through intellectual problems for themselves. It'd be terrific if you had a Socrates to help you draw out all the lessons from your decades of emotional experience.

The assumption behind giving lectures is that telling is teaching. It can be, but lecturing is not the best method of teaching.

The Socratic method is the best method of teaching. It's really the method used by the best one-on-one coaches. Let's assume for the sake of this topic that I am your emotions coach. Of course, for other topics, you may be my coach. In this case, however, I'm at least supposed to be the expert and you're the student.

The task is this: to transfer my understanding to you as effectively and efficiently as possible. The most skillful way to do that would be to use the Socratic method.

Effectively used in a conversation back and forth, it would ensure that what I'm saying would be perfectly pitched to your level of understanding. Being an expert makes it easy to talk over peoples' heads. For example, if I were a physicist trying to explain quantum mechanics and addressing a group of elementary school students the same way I'd normally address a group of undergraduate physics majors, I'd accomplish nothing worthwhile.

If I were addressing a group of undergraduate physics majors the same way I'd normally address a group of elementary school students, I'd also accomplish nothing worthwhile.

The most skillful way would be to adjust how I'm presenting the content to the level of understanding of the audience. The idea would be to stretch their understanding to enable them to learn without stretching it too much.

Ideally, instead of talking to a group, when teaching it's always better to have a conversation with one student. That's the easiest way to increase the odds of teaching someone something well.

The best way to do that would be (i) to find out what that student already understands and then (ii) to build upon it using analogies familiar to that student, in other words, by pointing out relevant similarities and differences between the new content that you're trying to teach and the content that that student already understands.

In this way, the best teachers test for and develop competence. The practical takeaway whenever you're teaching something is to find out what your students already understand and then build on that experience to extend it in fresh ways. As a practical matter in our educational system, it would generally be too expensive to have students taught one-on-one by experts, so we teach them in groups instead.

Here, though, it's just the two of us. What I'm trying to do is to draw upon your own experience so that you'll quickly come to understand what may be new content to you.

What's your own experience? Obviously, I don't know. I assume, though, that you've many times experienced negative emotions such as fear and positive emotions such as happiness. That's the raw experience you've had whose benefits we'd both like to maximize.

As much as possible, please initially assume that I really am an expert with respect to emotional well-being. In other words, set aside – at least for now – your own thoughts about emotional well-being whenever they happen to disagree with mine. If you don't, they'll just obstruct you from learning anything new about emotional well-being.

There's nothing to fear: if you should later decide that I'm not what I claim to be, then simply go back to your old beliefs about emotional well-being. In fact, you'll be able to return to them with more confidence than ever because you'll have tested them and they'll have survived that challenge. So, that'd be a win for you.

On the other hand, if you decide that the content about emotional well-being that I'm offering you is better and more valuable than what you used to believe, replace your old beliefs with your new and better ones. So, that would also be a win for you.

Having an open mind is critical. If your mind is closed, you have the mind of a fanatic.

There's a simple reason why that's foolish: it's that the world is always in flux. If your beliefs are static while the world is changing, the gap between your beliefs and reality is increasing rather than decreasing. That's a recipe for disaster. It's blocks learning from experience and explains why it's always foolish to be fanatically stuck on beliefs.

This explains why the very loving Francis of Assisi, who was a 13th century saint (sage, someone wise), advised us to "wear the world as a loose garment." Always be ready to shed beliefs as if they were loose garments.

Being a philosopher is the only alternative to being a fanatic. Etymologically, the word 'philosopher' means 'lover of wisdom.' Since someone who is wise lives well, the goal of all philosophers is to live well.

Not all philosophers succeed. In fact, most may fail. Nevertheless, unlike fanatics, even those who actually fail are open to success and mastery. Furthermore, some do succeed. Successful philosophers are sages (saints, those who are wise). An open mind is a noble mind. When we open our minds, when we set aside attachment to all our favorite beliefs, we open the genuine possibility of improving our lives.

It's true that philosophy isn't popular. Keep in mind that nonphilosophers literally killed Socrates. Furthermore, obviously, practicing philosophy, living an examined life, is dangerous to one's old beliefs. At least until they become wise, philosophers deliberately separate themselves from fanatics by being willing to question **all** their own beliefs.

Yes, I mean "all." If you have beliefs that you refuse to question, you are being a fanatic. If, for example, you have such favorite political or religious beliefs, you're being fanatical (radical, a true believer).

As the Buddha remarked, it's fanatics who go around bothering other people starting wars and other conflicts. It's not philosophers who break the peace. Philosophers seek peaceful lives without conflicts.

Where do you stand? I don't know. I shall, though, assume that you're a philosopher willing to question your own beliefs about emotions. If that assumption is wrong, your reading the rest of this would be useless. Might as well stop now.

I think you'd be wise to question your own beliefs. I think you'd be wise to question all your own beliefs.

By all means question all the beliefs that I offer in this book. The quality of our lives is a direct reflection of the quality of our questioning. That's just the way life is. Let's consider more about the way that we discover life to be.

The Buddha wasn't just a great thinker. He was a great human being, a sage.

In fact, he never wrote any books and one reason for that may have been that he didn't want people attaching to his thoughts. (Although Plato, who was the first great philosopher in the western tradition as the Buddha was the first great philosopher in the eastern tradition, did write books, his was a similar tale because he wrote dialogues rather than monologues. Why? Presumably, he wanted to encourage others to participate indirectly in them in order to burst their own conceptual limitations.) Instead, the Buddha always instructed his students to find out for themselves. He encouraged them to get beyond thoughts into their lives by practicing well. Meditation was the chief practice he recommended. This brings us to the idea of taking refuge.

To interpret the idea of taking refuge correctly, instead of thinking of a refuge as a safe haven, think of it as a commitment. Taking refuge involves a continuing sequence of decisions to throw oneself unreservedly into practice-enlightenment. In Invoking Reality, Loori uses the analogy of a child taking refuge in a parent's arms — but think of the child as being at a dangerous height need- ing to jump to be caught by the parent. The child must trust unequivocally to jump, and, once the child jumps, there's no taking the leap back. Similarly, Kierkegaard promotes the value of a continuing leap of faith. Like the child, we, too, fear the consequences of taking refuge, of plunging wholeheartedly into practice-enlightenment, of letting go of all our many attachments, so we hesitate— at least until our realization of how much we are suffering and causing others around us to suffer provides a sufficient goad. The Buddha encourages us to realize four facts of life if we would be noble and live well.

The **first** truth is that living is difficult, imperfect, flawed. Usually our lives are persistently and pervasively unsatisfactory. Sometimes our suffering is acute; sometimes we are on fire. Often, though, the misery is routine. Even moments of happiness are transitory and have a bittersweet quality; knowing they will soon end, we desperately cling to them. It's not as if our lives flow smoothly from one joyful experience to the next. Humiliation awaits each of us. Who among us is exempt from decay and illness? Who among us won't suffer the infirmities of age? Who among us won't die? Who among us has established loving encounters that are permanent? We are humiliated by being unable to control our destinies.

The **second** truth is that it is our egoistic attachments, our narcissistic cravings, that make life difficult. As we continually ask of life what it cannot give, as we incessantly try to control what isn't in our power to control, as we are buffeted by one obsessive thirst after another, we hurt. It's our selfish desires that are causing us to suffer. It is our incessant delusive quest for permanent pleasure that opens us to suffering. This is why living is difficult. The limited egoic mind is the source of suffering.

The **third** truth is that we have the option to liberate ourselves from life's difficulties. Freedom from our egoistic attachments, our narcissistic cravings, is possible. We can eliminate all the sorrow and suffering by eliminating what is causing the suffering. If we dissolve our egoism and our selfish desires, if we detach from our familiar attachments and live in a nonattached way, we'll discover that we lack nothing. The more we deliberately counteract our normal psychological conditioning, the more peace we'll enjoy. There really is a way to end our difficulties that will create lasting well-being.

The **fourth** truth is that the way to realize this liberation is the eightfold Path of: right view, right thinking, right mindfulness, right speech, right action, right diligence, right concentration, and right livelihood. By cultivating a compassionate life of virtue, wisdom, and meditation, we are able to realize our inherent enlightenment. Living this path is living well. This is wisdom, living as sages live.

Notice that this is not an accomplishment in the sense that it's something we gain or achieve; rather, it's a letting go of all the egoistic attachments that are blocking us from realizing our inherent nature. In that sense, living well is living while constantly surrendering to reality.

3:

Removing a Critical Obstacle

So, the Buddha recommends meditation. Permit me to emphasize how much he recommends it and why he recommends it. [All quotes in this chapter are from Easwaran's translation of The Dhammapada.]

Then, in case you are not already doing it daily, I explain the easiest way to begin. The sooner you begin meditating, the sooner you'll undermine emotional distress and begin living better with more ease.

What's the foundational problem? Ignorance. We do not know how to be and what to do to live well. "[T]here is no impurity greater than ignorance."

If we knew what we were doing, we'd do it. That is one of Socrates's great insights. There's no such thing as moral backsliding. If so, the question becomes, "How do we eliminate ignorance?" We need to purify our minds. "Make your mind pure as a silversmith blows away the impurities of silver, little by little." This means deliberately and repeatedly detaching from thoughts, in other words, emptying the mind.

Have you ever noticed how all thoughts insist on their importance? They are all rather like crying babies trying to attract attention. However, it is that undisciplined attention that creates the problem. Instead of living fully in the moment, we are separated from doing that by paying attention to whatever thoughts happen to arise. What sense does it make to think that we could possibly live well without even paying attention to what's going on right now? It makes no sense at all.

This is the problem that meditation cures. It's simple to understand: "Meditation brings wisdom; lack of meditation leaves ignorance." Foolish people don't meditate and, so, never become wise. "There can be no meditation for those who are not wise, and no wisdom for those who do not meditate." A genuine practitioner "meditates deeply, is at peace . . . and lives in joy."

The choice is simple: **either meditate or give up the idea of ever living well.**

Can't we, for example, earn our way to salvation? No, because "no amount of penance can help a person whose mind is not purified." The purpose of meditation is to purify the mind. It's not easy. "Hard it is to train the mind." However, it's worth it because "a trained mind brings health and happiness. . . They are wise whose thoughts are steady and minds serene . . ." Being wise is being happy and peaceful. The wise "are awake and free from fear. . . they attain the highest joy and freedom."

This is impossible without freedom from unwanted emotions (passions, agitations) like fear. It's impossible to be serene when our emotions are riled up and our thoughts are agitated. The Buddha is quite clear about this. Purifying (training, disciplining) the mind properly results in peacefulness. This includes purifying or emptying the mind of all emotions or passions. "As rain seeps through an ill-thatched hut, passion will seep through an untrained mind. As rain cannot seep through a well-thatched hut, passion cannot seep through a well-trained mind."

Haven't you at least occasionally experienced emotional overwhelm? Living that way is unnecessary. "If you meditate earnestly, through spiritual disciplines you can make an island for yourself that no flood can overwhelm."

For example, one of the worst human experiences is the death of a child. The Buddha's only child died before he did. When told of his son's death, what did the Buddha say and do? Did he cry out for unending weeks about his loss? Did he think that the rest of his life was ruined because of his misfortune? No. He accepted reality. He said nothing and didn't change how he was living.

There are many different kinds of meditation, many different spiritual disciplines (practices, trainings) to purify the mind. There's not one that works best for everyone. If you don't already have one that works well for you, it'll likely require some trial and error before you settle on one.

What about prayer? Absolute prayer, which aims at unity with the divine, is a spiritual discipline. It's prayer as mystics pray. [For more on this, see the "Prayers of Unity" video on the DENNIS BRADFORD PHD YouTube channel.] Most prayer, by way of contrast, is petitionary and, so, self-centered; instead of dissolving attachment to the ego, it actually strengthens it. Instead of dissolving egoistic attachments, it actually strengthens them. Although they can overlap, it's a mistake to confuse a spiritual practice with a religious one.

If we don't meditate, it's impossible for our lives to improve significantly. We'll just continue in our separate ways to have our gains and losses, our highs and lows, our rewards and punishments, until, if we are lucky, we grow old, become ill, and die. There will be neither abiding serenity nor genuine love [See my Love and Respect].

Always, one must pay the price. There is an opportunity cost with respect to meditation; if you're meditating properly, you cannot simultaneously be, for example, thinking about how to solve problems. If your meditative practice is a stilling one, you cannot be doing anything else such as cleaning the house, raking leaves, or cooking. In that sense, finding the time to meditate can be a problem.

There are other problems as well. The most important one with respect to a stilling practice is physical pain. If you sit still for any length of time, you'll sooner or later experience pain. Alternatively or additionally, you may feel lazy, drowsy, or sleepy.

The very thoughts from which you are trying to free yourself may increase in intensity. You may become restless or worried. You may experience desire for something else. Feelings of ill will may arise as well as doubts that meditation is even worth doing. You may realize that you're a slave to your thoughts and are unable to stop thinking. Delusive thoughts can increase and apparently buried feelings may arise. Anxiety and depression can increase rather than decrease. You may wonder what you are doing sitting there instead of being out trying to save the world.

All these thoughts can lead you simply to drop the idea of meditating at all. However, if the Buddha is right that there's no living well without meditating, that can also lead to feelings of guilt or shame. In fact, the best way to save the world is to begin by saving yourself, which means emptying the mind to awaken spiritually.

There is no problem associated with meditation that cannot be overcome. Every normal human being is able to meditate successfully. What, though, if you are suffering acutely and, so, are at least temporarily sub-normal? [I have discussed this in other places such as in Introduction to Living Well and Are You Living

<u>Without Purpose?</u>] If you're suffering acutely, don't worry about acquiring a meditative practice just yet. Instead, get some help and first get back to normal; once there, then you may begin meditating. In the long run, nothing will help you more than meditation.

Permit me to suggest what my experience of teaching many people how to meditate over the years is the best way for most people to begin to meditate. There's no better way to meditate in the sense that no other kind of meditation is as free of potential problems. It's the least painful stilling meditation. Since it's a stilling meditation, it can be learned quickly. It doesn't require expending physical energy. In short doses of, say, 20 minutes, it's pain free. It alleviates stress. It's very enjoyable, too.

As usual, there's no standard terminology here. Let's call it "aliveness awareness" and simply note that it has other names as well such as "energy awareness" or "life energy awareness."

What's the best way to think about it? **Aliveness awareness is a way of vacationing!**

Our English word 'vacation' comes from a French verb that means 'to vacate.' To vacate what? To vacate the mind of thoughts and emotions, especially troubling thoughts and emotions.

When you think of a vacation, perhaps you think of visiting the seashore or going camping in the mountains. Have you ever gone on a vacation only to find that you dragged all your troubles with you and then returned from your vacation feeling no more refreshed than when it began?

Isn't the chief purpose of a vacation to free yourself temporarily from your problems? If all you do on vacation is to keep thinking about your problems, there cannot be any reset or freedom from them even temporarily.

Why do you often seem to have such difficulty not thinking about your problems? It's because you don't practice detaching from them. How could you become non-attached to problems if you never detach from them?

Whatever we focus on becomes more important. Therefore, the more you focus on your problems, the more important they become. Think of your daily periods of aliveness awareness as short vacations in which you detach from thinking about all your problems. Every time you practice letting go of thoughts, you are vacationing well, relaxing. Why not at least take multiple vacations daily? I do, and that's what I recommend. *Aliveness awareness is a skill.* The more you practice it, the better you'll become at it. By virtue of being human you already have the aptitude for it. So, permit me to describe how to do it and then answer a few questions that may occur to you about it.

It could not be simpler: just *do as little as possible!* That sounds like a vacation, right? Permit me to describe it both physically and mentally.

Still yourself physically. This is how to begin practicing aliveness awareness. You're going to be comfortable and perfectly still for 5 minutes, 20 minutes, or however long you're going to practice.

Since you're less likely to be bothered by inclement weather, insects or other animals, human-made noises, or other people, it's easier if you're inside rather than outside. A quiet room where you feel safe is best.

It works best if you're able to lie back. If you're fortunate enough to have a comfortable recliner in a quiet room, use that. Simply lie back on the recliner. Do not cross your legs; keep them relaxed and together. Have your upper arms next to your torso. Relax your hands either on top of your hips or next to them, whichever is more comfortable. Ensure that you neck is straight and relaxed.

It's easiest for a beginner to focus if you close your eyelids, but that's not mandatory. If you don't, keep your eyes still and, if possible, let them go out of focus. (That's unnecessary after you get good at aliveness awareness.)

Take a deep breath or two to help you relax. Your breathing should soon naturally become silent, regular, deep, and slow. Don't force it to do anything; let it be natural. Don't talk.

In short, simply *lie back in a comfortable position* that's easy to sustain for a while. Stilling yourself physically really is simple, isn't it?

Still yourself mentally. This is really what any kind of meditation is all about. Don't think of it as trying to gain something; instead, think of losing the heavy burden of your thoughts, which includes all the unsolved problems you worry about and carry around with you as well as all the emotions they spawn. Rather than think of meditation as adding supposedly beneficial thoughts to the mind, think of meditation as emptying thoughts from the mind. If you want more thoughts, read a book or take a course. If you want more peace of mind, meditate. Let go of all thoughts.

That's the key to feeling better emotionally. [I explain exactly how that occurs in Chapter 7.] There's no need to belief anything with one exception, namely, simply believe that aliveness awareness *might* help you live better. It's very unlike having to swallow a religious creed.

Detaching from thoughts successfully leads to nonattachment, which not only is peace of mind but enables engaged action when life requires it. Although you may not yet be ready either to understand or to accept it, the reason this works is because **you already are what you need to be to live well.**

Aliveness awareness is not only simple, but it's easily mastered. Just still the body as described above and then, as much as possible, still the mind by focusing on the aliveness in the body. That aliveness is right here right now.

The reason you may have never noticed it is that you are addicted to compulsive thinking, incessant "thoughting."

You have a working brain that is constantly generating thoughts to which you pay attention. What you'll now be practicing is *not* paying attention to thoughts by paying attention instead to aliveness.

By focusing on the sensations of aliveness from your still body, you'll automatically be letting go of thoughts as they arise. That's the key: *as soon as you notice a thought, drop it in favor of paying attention to the aliveness.* Meditation is just that simple. However, what's simple is not necessarily easy.

Aliveness awareness is just a way to make detachment from compulsive thinking easier.

Physical objects are ultimately shimmering clumps of energy. If you've ever cared over time for a house or an automobile, you already understand that they deteriorate as time goes by. Bodies never stay the same – and that goes for your body as well. As you've likely noticed, your body is aging. It's actually in incessant flux.

Focusing on its aliveness is drawing attention away from thoughts. Notice that it's not actually paying attention to the body itself but to its aliveness. It's a direct experience of that aliveness that bypasses the intellect. The more we do it, the weaker identification with our bodies becomes. You are much, much more than just a living body, more than just an animal.

Aliveness awareness is enjoyable. Simply being alive feels good. The reason that we usually don't notice that is because we're lost in thought, living in our heads.

Here's how to correct that: become aware of the life energy in your motionless hands. Don't think about the life energy in them. Don't ask your intellect if there is life energy in your hands. Just focus on the life energy that already is in your still hands.

If you notice nothing at first, don't worry or think about that at all. Just keep paying attention. Keep practicing daily for a few minutes until you begin to feel it. Don't worry: it's there! We know that because you're alive.

The longer it takes you to feel it, the more you need this practice. Sooner or later you'll notice a slight tingling in them. It feels something like a very mild and pleasant electrical sensation.

Extend your focus in sequence to various other parts of your body such as your feet, legs, arms, stomach, chest, face, and so on. Eventually, you'll be able to experience the aliveness throughout your body.

Practice this every day. Soon you may not have to close your eyes or keep them still or even be still physically to feel it. Make this exercise into a habit. It's not only a way of feeling more alive in the present moment, but also it's a way of getting beyond the prison of conceptual thinking. **Instead of permitting your attention to go wherever it wants to go, you will discipline [purify, train] awareness to focus on the aliveness of your body.**

Permit me to answer a few common questions that beginning practitioners sometimes have.

How long does it take until I'm able to experience the aliveness? This varies. You may feel it immediately or it may take you weeks of trying it for a few minutes daily. The more you're able to focus well, the more quickly you'll begin to enjoy feeling the aliveness.

How long did it take you? I committed myself to doing it for 5 minutes daily until I could begin to feel it. It took about 2 weeks until I initially felt it in a knuckle of one hand.

What if I'm unable to feel anything? Persist until success. Every cell in your body is alive and, now that you know about it, it'd be foolish to go through life without enjoying aliveness sensations. It's impossible to fail unless you quit, so just don't quit and you won't fail. It's not as if being still for a few minutes daily will hurt or injure you. It's restful and beneficial anyway.

What should I do when I begin to feel it? Extend it to other parts of your body. In my case, I extended it from one knuckle to one finger and then to that whole hand. Next, I focused on "opening up" the other hand. Then I switched to my feet. (Many people find it easier to begin focusing on their feet rather than focusing on their hands.) Then I went up the shins and thighs. I went up each forearm to each upper arm. Eventually, I extended it to my face and torso.

Should I time my practice sessions? It's a good idea initially. Why? If you fail to time your practice sessions, you'll begin thinking about their length. You'll sometimes wonder, "How much longer?" If you use a timer, there'll be no need to think about their length. An ordinary kitchen timer or cell phone that makes an audible sound is fine – but don't have it so near you that it jars you when it goes off.

What are the best times to practice? Because **all classic meditative practices are nurturing practices,** any time is a good time to practice.

When beginning a new practice of any kind, usually the best time to begin any new practice is first thing in the morning before your excuses for not practicing have a chance to pile up. It doesn't matter if you practice aliveness awareness before or after coffee or tea. It really doesn't matter if you practice before or after breakfast or any other meal. The point is to make practicing part of your everyday morning routine just like brushing your teeth.

Another excellent time to practice is just before you go to bed – and do NOT watch any electronic devices such as computers, smart phones, or televisions after practicing.

A third excellent time to practice is after the workday is over and before dinner.

What's the goal of aliveness awareness? It's a mistake to think that you are trying to achieve or gain anything by meditating. The point is not to attach to something new. The point is *non*attachment from thoughts. You'll lose stress, anxiety, and emotional disturbances. The practice itself is not only simple and easy, but it's physically enjoyable and sustainable (although after an hour or so you may get a bit stiff).

If you're thinking about goals, you're thinking. It's impossible to think and to meditate simultaneously. The Third Ancestor in the Ch'an [Chinese Zen] tradition says bluntly, "The wise do not strive after goals." [Rochester Zen Center translation] All goals are to be achieved in the future. Anything involving the future inherently involves thinking. Where, outside thought, is the future? The future has no reality outside thinking. The more you think about the future, the more you miss life in the present. <u>Complete acceptance of what is right now just as it is is complete peace of mind.</u>

What's the point of detaching from thoughts? Freedom from compulsive thinking, which obstructs the direct experience of reality. A good way to explain this is with respect to stress. Whether physical or mental, stress is always the result of opposing forces. With respect to physical stress, aliveness awareness is so relaxing that you may fall asleep easily! With respect to mental stress, all kinds of meditation reduce it because, again, of the psychological law that **the more we pay attention to something the more valuable it becomes.** Life only occurs in the present moment; it's impossible to live yesterday now or to live tomorrow now. Thoughts are almost always about either the past, the future, or elsewhere. To focus on aliveness is to focus less on thoughts. The more we do that, the more fully we are present now. Since mental stress results from opposed thoughts, the less we attend to the relevant thoughts, the less stress we experience. When we are not attached to any thoughts, *all* mental stress dissolves and we experience complete freedom from mental stress. That's being peaceful, isn't it?

All classic meditative practices promote peacefulness. They all promote nonattachment. Unlike detachment that can seem like a deadening withdrawal from life, nonattachment permits full engagement with life in the present moment without distraction. Most people yearn to live more fully and enjoy greater satisfaction. Meditation is how to do that.

Daily life is not as serious a most people think it is. If you really want more fun and more play, meditate!

What if I don't have a recliner? That's not really a problem. If you have a bed, lie back on it. If not, lie on the floor or on the ground. If you use a flat surface, it's best to put a pillow or rolled up blanket or something similar under your knees to take the strain off your lower back. If you're more comfortable with a pillow also under the back of your head, that's not a problem.

Conditions don't have to be perfect for you to begin practicing.

How long should I practice every day? All meditative practices are nurturing practices. The more you practice, the better you'll feel. Until you begin to feel the aliveness, I recommend a minimum of 5 minutes daily. You may do that several times daily if you want. After you begin feeling the aliveness, that itself will provide motivation for you to continue and to open up different parts of your body. When you're enjoying the aliveness throughout your body, you'll want to experience it for at least 20 or 30 minutes twice daily. You'll look forward to it.

After a few weeks, what will happen is that, whenever you are physically still, you'll begin feeling the aliveness when you aren't even deliberately practicing. That's a sign that you are well on your way to realizing for yourself that master meditators are always meditating.

May I skip a practice session? Of course you may. The meditation police are not going to come to your home and arrest you! Should you? No. The key when learning to master a new skill is: **never skip practicing**. As the Buddha said, "Any indiscipline brings evil in its wake." Many times when learning a new skill you will seem to be on a plateau rather than improving. As long as you don't think that's a problem, it's not a problem.

Most practice sessions do not result in noticeable jumps in the skill. Most practice sessions do not show any improvement. Therefore, there's a sense in which *the key to mastery is to enjoy the plateaus of practicing.* Don't let thoughts of increased future mastery intrude. Be fully here right now. Be assured that, if you are working on the practice, the practice is working on you.

Don't think about practicing. Don't evaluate practice sessions. Just practice. The Buddha: "Let go of the past! / Let go of the future! / In the present, let go!"

4:

Cleansing Consciousness

The world is in incessant flux. That requires relentlessly adapting to changing circumstances. The more creatively we adapt, the better we live. Becoming more creative is not only required for solving life's challenges, but also being creative can be extremely rewarding.

How may we become more creative?

The best way to increase creativity is (i) to understand where it comes from and then deliberately (ii) dissolve obstacles to becoming more creative.

Don't limit yourself only to thinking about producing what is new; it's also important to develop ingenious ways to preserve that which is good and to destroy that which is bad. The idea is to work out novel, game-changing solutions that are "outside the box."

Creative geniuses can leave us dumbstruck with awe. Think of Michelangelo and Picasso, Aeschylus and Shakespeare,

Mozart and Beethoven, Dostoevsky and Tolstoy, Plato and Aristotle, Darwin and Einstein. The idea of emulating them in becoming more creative may strike you as madness.

However, every field has its innovators. It's easy to see in athletics. If you are, like me, a hockey fan, you understand how Bobby Orr and Wayne Gretzky changed the game. Where would baseball be without Babe Ruth? How thrilling it was to watch Bill Russell and Michael Jordan play basketball! If you don't think Bill Belichick comes up with innovative solutions to coaching problems year after year, you simply don't follow pro football.

Go to any department in a university and enquire about that field's greats. Look behind any successful business and you'll find an inspiring story. There are even creative captains of war from Alexander the Great to Douglas MacArthur.

Think of the people you know who are consistently creative. How do they do it?

Creativity comes from no-thought. What's that? How is it practiced?

Winston Churchill: "Remember the story of the Spanish prisoner. For many years he was confined in a dungeon . . . One day it occurred to him to push the door of his cell. It was open; and it had never been locked."

Until we break free, we're all prisoners of our own conceptual systems, our own particular ways of understanding, our own intellectual prisons. Creativity requires breaking free from our usual ways of thinking.

Have you ever been stuck for a long time on a particular problem when, all of a sudden, its solution occurred to you? Although you weren't able to think deliberately of a solution, perhaps while you were showering or waking up or enjoying a walk, the solution just popped suddenly into your awareness.

That's how creative solutions occur: they just appear after letting our brains mull over problems. That's why becoming more creative is really a matter of letting go of the usual ways of thinking that keep us bound. Instead of becoming stuck and recycling the same stale old thoughts, creativity involves letting go of them and approaching life without our usual fetters. It's a burst of intellectual evolution.

If you're familiar with creativity in the fine arts, you already understand this. If you were, for example, a master painter, you could relatively easily teach a student how to master its techniques. What you couldn't do directly, however, is to teach a student how to paint creatively.

Fortunately, there are a number of techniques that indirectly can help us become more creative. The best one I know is "**morning pages**." It's simple and effective. Here's how to think about it and how to do it.

There are two kinds of episodes of consciousness, namely, "thought" and "no-thought" or "thinking" and "awareness."

Thought or thinking is conceptualizing. It's about separating into categories (sorting, classifying, dividing, discriminating). Discursive thinking is essential to survival. Unless we are able successfully to discriminate, for example, "food" from "not food" or "friend" from "enemy" or "benign" from "dangerous," we don't survive long.

As we live, we find some ways of thinking work better for us than others. Naturally, in novel situations, we tend to rely on what has worked in the past. When our daily situations become routine, so does the quality of our thinking. When we are literate, as most of us are, these ways of thinking become fossilized in writing. Once written down, thoughts are forever. Reading books and listening to others talk can be enormously helpful with respect to thinking well. That's the way of thought.

Always, again, one must pay the price. What's the downside of the way of thought?

Concepts, principles of classification, are static, lifeless, inert. Once we master them it's easy to get stuck thinking. In fact, most people are stuck in thought most of their waking lives. Instead of living in their lives, they are living in their thoughts!

That's not living well. It's living in a conceptual prison, living in a box.

Noting this is not to deny that being able to think well is a helpful asset. As Hume pointed out, habit is the great flywheel of our lives. It's not just that our behaviors are usually repetitive, it's that our thoughts are as well.

However useful and comfortable, repetition is the enemy of creativity.

Fortunately, unless we kill it, we seem to have a natural antipathy to living in a lifeless box.

Here's a quick test: Are you someone who finds the world dead with the resulting problem that life is difficult to explain or are you someone who finds the world living with the resulting problem that stasis is difficult to explain? In this age of literacy, most of us naturally fall into the former camp.

Thought creates inequalities, whereas no-thought dissolves them. This is because evaluations are thoughts. If we are continually thinking "this is good for me" or "this is bad for me" about the contents of our minds, we are automatically running all experiences through out conceptual systems and, so, deadening them. This is why day-to-day living can often feel stale and boring. The way to revive natural freshness is to let go of thought.

Emerson noted that "it is so much easier to do what one has done before than to do a new thing, that there is a perpetual tendency to a set mode." Staying in "set mode" is the obstacle to living in "creative mode."

In the abstract domain of thought, everything is dead, whereas in the living natural domain of no-thought, as Emerson noted, "Nothing is dead." Think of being fully alive to the present moment. Think of an episode when your life flowed. It may have been while you were playing a musical instrument or a sport. It may have been in an emergency situation when there was no time for thought. It may have been when you were "in the zone" acting without thought but perfectly appropriately and masterfully. That's **no-thought**, alert awareness without thought.

Yes, thought is useful and necessary, but unless we deliberately minimize it, our lives become boring, dull, and uninteresting. To avoid this, many seek endless distractions such as the popular drugs, sex, and rock n roll used by most teenagers.

The solution is to set aside thought regularly, which automatically diminishes the conceptual deadness that can spoil so much of life. Setting thoughts aside automatically unleashes creativity.

The bad news is that most of us are seriously underdeveloped when it comes to no-thought.

The good news is that, if so, noticing this opens up an important opportunity: we are all able to become more creative by practicing no-thought more frequently. Fortunately, there are many ways to do that.

Furthermore, *opening up creativity for one purpose automatically opens it up for other purposes*. Mastering any of the available, effective methods of creativity training typically improves life in multiple ways. They are therefore different from mastering specific skills such as, say, playing the flute or firing a slap shot in hockey. Skills like those are not transferable to other domains.

Nevertheless, because they are more common, specific skills are better examples of no-thought than general skills like meditation. Think of one that you yourself have practiced properly for so long that you mastered it, that you transitioned from the thought characteristic of a beginner to the no-thought characteristic of a master. You've probably done that many times.

Consider walking for example. You don't remember how long you struggled to learn how to walk, but you may be able to ask your parents. You tried and failed, tried and failed, tried and failed many, many times. With persistent practice of the right kind you eventually were able to emulate all those giants who were walking all around you. Now you're a master walker. Unless you're injured, you're able to do it automatically and well.

In fact, you do it so automatically that you are usually busy thinking of something other than your walking while you are walking, right? N.B.: That's an example of **separation**, which **is the root of suffering**.

Let's consider a case where you're <u>only</u> walking, in other words, walking with no-thought. It's a crisp fall day and you're walking up a forested hill. You are not following a path; you are blazing your own trail. This hill is sufficiently steep that you are sometimes more climbing than walking. You are fully focused on what you are doing.

You are not, however, thinking about it. You simply feel each step underfoot. You pay full attention to which branch to grab and how best to detour around certain large rocks. You're aware of an occasional insect or rivulet of sweat trickling down your back. You cross openings during which the sun feels warm and a breeze caresses you.

Isn't that an everyday example of creativity? What could thought add to that experience?

Incidentally, if you usually paid attention to each step like that, you would be practicing walking meditation. Instead of being lost in thought imagining what will happen when you reach your future destination, you would be fully feeling each step. Instead of assuming that the future moment will be better than the present moment, your attention would be fully engaged in the now.

Instead of living in the present moment, thought casts us into what we hope will be a better future. That's why we often crave living more deeply: we miss a lot of our lives. After all, our lives only ever occur here and now; they never occur in the future or in the past or elsewhere. We miss life whenever we think about something else. That's why living better requires doing less thinking.

Instead of thinking of the present as nothing but a momentary transition from what was to what will be, creativity only occurs in the fullness of the present moment. Therefore, if you deliberately practice no-thought in order to enhance your creativity, don't be surprised if you begin feeling more satisfied with your life overall.

So: how may be become more creative?

Here's how to train yourself to become more creative. It's not only simple, but it's also effective. It's based on the idea of emptying the mind of surplus thoughts where attention frequently gets stuck, of cleansing (draining, flushing) the mind.

Every morning, sit down at a well-lit table with some notebook paper and a couple of pens. *On a minimum of one side of 3 pieces of paper, write down your thoughts.* When you are done, put the paper in your notebook and don't look at it for at least 90 days and don't share it before then with anyone else. That's it!

There's no trick to it. Writing down thoughts will free you from having to think about them. Commit to doing it for 90 days without fail. Test this procedure well for yourself.

There are no content requirements. You may write about anything. You may find that you have grievances or complaints or gripes; if so, write them down. You may find that you are thinking about the weather; if so, write down your thoughts about it. If you get stuck, write about getting stuck. You may write about your fears and frustrations. You may write about your hopes and fantasies. You may write about anything you are thinking about.

Do write by hand using a pen or pencil. Do fill up 3 sheets of paper. I like college-ruled, 3-hole notebook paper, but use whatever kind of paper you prefer. The only requirement is that you, in effect, flush out of your mind whatever your thoughts happen to be so that you can start the day with something like a cleansed consciousness. Set your internal self-critic aside for a few minutes. It's stream-of-consciousness writing. If possible, try to get into a state of flow, which is an optimal experience and wholly enjoyable.

This morning pages technique (method, procedure) is not original. I learned it from The Artist's Way by Julia Cameron with Mark Bryan, which I recommend. If you practice, it's like beginning each day by giving yourself an important gift.

Whether your writing flows or not, do not stand up until you have filled up at least 3 pages. As always when learning a new skill, do not skip practicing. Except for grave illness or injury, there are no acceptable excuses. Just do it.

The more difficult you find this practice, the more you need to unleash your creativity.

This practice is a wonderful complement to aliveness awareness.

5:

What You Already Understand About Emotions

O ur goal is to kill unwanted emotions when they arise or to prevent them from arising initially so that we may diminish and eliminate emotional suffering. Our goal is to end emotional distress. Our goal is to flourish emotionally.

We all have so many beliefs that it's impossible to question them all singly. This is why great philosophers like Descartes recommend questioning them in bunches. So let's question beliefs about the nature and value of emotions.

The answers I recommend may be, however unfamiliar, quite beneficial. You'll decide that for yourself after understanding them. Let's focus here on the beliefs you already have about emotions. Let's begin by setting them aside in order to gain perspective on them. Since a closed mind can't learn, resolve to open to what may well be ideas about emotions that are new to you. Have no fear: you may return to your former ideas later if you want, but I don't think you'll want to do that.

Recalling your own emotional experiences and setting aside at least temporarily all your general beliefs about emotions, what do I recommend with respect to emotional well-being and what's the justification for those recommendations?

When gardening well, weeding and soil preparation should come before seeding.

It's the same when we're thinking about a category of beliefs. If you have at least temporarily (and courageously!) adopted the open-minded attitude of a philosopher about emotions, let's examine your own emotional experience. In the next chapter, let's identify and delete 6 common myths or false beliefs about emotions that, if you cling to them, will obstruct your emotional progress.

Since I don't know you personally, I cannot be sure what your emotional experience has been. So, I'll simply assume that it's been similar to my own.

What lessons have I learned from my own experience about emotions? Here are 9 major lessons, and I've added a 10th that all experts agree on. I assume that we're in agreement about them. In other words, we'll start by reviewing 10 common beliefs about emotions that are correct.

All emotions are disruptions, disturbances. They all upset serenity, peace of mind. This is central. In fact, the English word 'emotion' derived from a French word meaning a mental agitation. Emotions are passions.

Thoughts are relevant to emotions. Anger, shame, guilt, fear, happiness, and other emotions are not somehow out there floating around in the atmosphere like germs that may happen to infect us. They are somehow intimately connected to our worldviews, which are embedded in our conceptual systems.

A "*concept*" is a principle of classification. If you're able to separate red objects from non-red objects, you have the concept of redness. A "*conceptual system*" is a hierarchy of concepts arranged in terms of generality. With respect to redness, for example, it has lower categories or species such as being pink or being crimson and it itself falls into higher categories such as being colored or being qualitied.

It's important to understand this if only because it explains why it's foolish to attach to any thought or conceptualization: *all conceptualizations are perspectival, partial, incomplete.* There's always an alternative way of applying concepts. From a purely logical point of view, this is why fanaticism is idiotic. It's logically impossible for any conceptualization to be the whole truth. Therefore, none deserves fanatical attachment.

Emotions are not just mental; they're also bodily. Thoughts are mental. Again, beliefs are just thoughts we accept as true. Emotions, though, have a physical or physiological component. They're not merely thoughts or beliefs. They connect our minds and our bodies. Although they can be experienced in any part of the body, intense emotions are often felt as sensations in the front of the body such as in the throat, chest, or gut.

"Minds" are nothing but mental contents such as thoughts, beliefs, images, and sensations.

There's a multiplicity of emotions. Some feel good and are positive; some hurt and are negative.

Since **an emotion is not the same as its consequences**, it's not the case that all positive emotions are good for us and it's not the case that all negative emotions are bad for us. For example, a positive emotion can distract us from doing something important and a negative emotion can prompt us to do something that will save our life.

Emotions vary in intensity and kinds. The same kind of emotion can vary in intensity. For example, anger can vary from the mild intensity of mere annoyance to the strong intensity of outright rage. The same kind of emotion can vary in kind. For example, anger can be cold or resentful or hot or indignant.

Emotions are motivators. They prepare us to act or behave in certain ways. For example, sufficient fear prompts the cascade of hormones known as the freeze, fight, or flight response.

Emotions often breed other emotions. For example, grief can lead to sadness, despondency, mourning, and remorse. Guilt can lead to anger and rage. Anger can lead to frustration and hatred. In fact, intense negative emotions are typically experienced in conjunction with other negative emotions. Individual emotions are slippery in that they often transform into related emotions and moods. (This is one reason why there is no generally agreed-upon list or categorization of emotions.)

Emotions are important. They are valuable. That's not only because they can prompt behaviors that are beneficial, but it's also because they can increase our enjoyment of life.

There are other general features of emotions that are well-known but not directly grounded in experience. I'll add the most important of these to the list: **emotions can kill**. They not only may have negative physiological consequences by weakening our immune systems, but they sometimes prompt murder as well as active and passive suicide. In other words, they can be necessary parts of causal sequences that lead to death.

Obviously, then, if preservation of life is desirable, it's a good idea to kill emotions. Why? Doing so removes one cause of death. I don't think that any of these ten features is controversial. That's true despite the fact that human beings differ in their susceptibility to emotions.

Even so, false beliefs about emotions abound. Despite the fact that they often have extremely deleterious effects on our lives, emotional myths are almost unbelievably popular. A chief reason for their popularity is that they promote the idea that we are not responsible for our emotions. Since emotions are important, it would follow that we are not responsible for an important part of our lives. Balderdash!

Let's examine popular myths about emotions.

6:

What You May Think You Already Understand About Emotions – But Don't

I've discussed emotional myths elsewhere in more detail. (Compare, for example, How to Survive College Emotionally and Emotional Facelift.) Permit me here simply to identify them and attempt to undermine each one quickly.

The situations myth is the idea that situations cause our emotions. Do you believe that? Even if you don't think you do, do you not infrequently act as if you do?

Do you ever catch yourself thinking or saying things such as: "He made me so angry!" "Her unexpected death made me so sad." "It surprised me that they won the championship." "That's disgusting!"

Believing that situations cause emotions has the very deleterious effect that we then spend a lot of life trying to improve our situations so that we'll feel better. How much of your life have you spent doing that? Do you spend a lot of time trying to make situations the way that you want them?

Situations occur. Stuff happens. We suffer losses as well as gains. That's true.

Ask: "Do situations cause emotions?" No, they do not. If they did, our emotional reactions to them would be similar, but they aren't.

When you heat water sufficiently to make a cup of tea, does it sometimes boil and sometimes not boil? No, the result is the same every time. It's rational to believe that the heat caused the water to boil.

Suppose you're a baseball fan and the Yankees just won the pennant again. How does that make you feel? Actually, it doesn't; that's a trick question. If you're a Yankee's fan, you'll feel good because you think it's good for you that they won the pennant. On the other hand, if you're not a Yankee's fan, you won't feel good because you think it's bad for you that they won the pennant.

There is no emotion necessarily connected to any situation. Instead, if there's a situation that we take to be relevant to us, we decide to feel good or bad about it. So, it would be alright to claim that situations are in the causal sequence that leads us to feel certain emotions, but it's false that situations by themselves cause emotions. Situations are always emotionally neutral.

Without your evaluations, you won't feel any emotions.

Do you find that accepting responsibility for your emotions is distressing? You shouldn't. Why? It means that *emotional suffering is optional!* Since you control what you believe and since the emotions that you feel depend upon those beliefs, you need not ever suffer emotionally. Enabling you to understand and do what's required to flourish emotionally is what this book is all about.

You should question this. After all, it's a common positionality that situations create emotions. The problem with continuing to believe it once it's questioned is based on the fact that all human beings are, although different, essentially similar in one respect, namely, we all want to be happy. So, we naturally behave in ways we hope will make us happy and in ways we hope will avoid making us unhappy.

However, different situations result in different emotions. If I'm a Yankee's fan and they win the pennant, I'll feel happy; if you hate the Yankees and they win the pennant, you'll feel unhappy. It's not what the Yankees did that causes my happiness and your unhappiness; instead, it the different ways that we react to what they did that makes the difference. There's nothing either emotionally good or emotionally bad about their winning the pennant except what we take to be emotionally good or bad about it. By themselves, situations are not laden with emotions.

This is why we don't need to change the world to be happy; we just sometimes need to change ourselves, specifically, our evaluations. When we drop them, we automatically lighten our emotional loads. We naturally enjoy life more because we become freer and more playful. [I return to this in Chapter 7.]

The myth of passivity is the idea that passivity is our only option whenever we experience unwanted emotions. Why? Supposedly, emotions pass over us without our consent rather like weather fronts, which we are powerless to control. Except to endure them until they dissipate, there's simply nothing we can do about them.

All myths are false beliefs that are servants of the ego. The myth of passivity is particularly vicious because, when taken to be true, it undermines the very possibility of emotional well-being.

Why believe it? It's easy to understand its purpose: it alleviates us of responsibility. When confronted with powerful unwanted emotions such as grief, shame, or fear, we are like helpless martyrs whose only choice is to die or to endure until the storm passes. Although it may be a noble effort, attempting to conquer such forces is hopeless.

Balderdash! Like behaviors, beliefs are actions. Who is in charge of how you act? You are. Nobody else could be. Unless your mind works in a wholly different way than mine does, what we do is up to us.

The belief in emotional helplessness is embedded in popular culture. For example, fear paralyzes us. Sadness distracts us. Annoyances anger us. Bloodlust disgusts us. Love is like falling into a pit. We are incessantly buffeted by forces beyond our control that make us feel in certain ways.

Before reading this, you may have uncritically accepted the myth of passivity. It only takes some accurate and careful thinking to undermine it quickly.

It's true that we are powerless to control many situations. It's also true that we may be conditioned to react to certain types of situations (for example, important losses) with certain emotions (for example, grief or sadness). Whatever we learn, however, can be surpassed or unlearned. Conditioned reactions can be broken and changed; we can recondition ourselves.

Own your conditioning. It's part of you. It's why emotions may seem involuntary. Accepting emotional responsibility is an important part of becoming mature. If you will religiously follow the practices promoted in this book, you may find that emotional maturity is not only more beneficial than you may have anticipated but also easier to attain than you may have anticipated.

Many who accept the myth of passivity also accept **the myth of innocence**, which is the idea that, before we critically examine them, emotions are valuable because they are free and natural. The <u>Bible</u> actually contains the idea that, the more we understand, the more we suffer.

More balderdash! Emotional innocence is nothing but emotional immaturity. <u>The situations that we become emotional about are the situations that we choose to become emotional about</u>. Not only is how we feel about those situations dependent upon how we understand them, in other words, the beliefs we accept, but also it's dependent upon the decisions we make involving them.

As Sartre notes, the alternative is senseless. How could something outside me decide for me how to be emotionally? I do emotions to myself. Although this may initially upset you, notice the great benefit of taking responsibility for the quality of your own emotional life, namely, you gain control over it. The emotionally immature *must* suffer emotionally. The emotionally mature have a choice.

Are you condemned to riding the emotional roller coaster up and down for the rest of your life? Not once you realize that you can get off it whenever you decide to get off it.

Notice that you cannot both be a slave to powerful emotions and also be free from them. The emotionally immature are slaves, and, so, lack freedom. Isn't freedom better than slavery?

If you ask people what techniques work to promote emotional maturity, many will respond with some form of **the myth that common tactics work**.

What are the common tactics that we often use? There's a continuum of tactics that range between the two extremes. Let's just consider here each extreme. Suppose that you are cursed with some powerful unwanted emotion or other. What might you try doing to free yourself?

Ignoring is one extreme tactic. It's an initially obvious option. Just go about your life as if you weren't feeling, for example, grief or rage or shame.

Even if it occasionally seems to work for weak emotions, you likely have tried it for powerful emotions and realized for yourself that it doesn't work. The reason that it doesn't work is simple: in order to ignore something, we have to be aware of it!

Even if that were possible, as any experienced psychiatrist or clinical psychologist will confirm, ignoring powerful negative emotions merely permits them to persist with the result that emotional poison may continue to seep into your life for years. In fact, that negative impact may only end with death. Unless you're suffering from self-hatred (which is just another unwanted emotion from which some people should free themselves), what's the point of enduring that condition when there's a clear alternative?

No loving mother ever raises her children to ignore powerful negative emotions. No mental health professional or other sane adult advises doing that either.

Venting is the other extreme tactic. It's the idea of acting out fueled by the emotion in question.

When you were a child and your little sister accidentally broke your favorite toy, did you react angrily and beat her up? If so, did that solve the problem? Of course not.

Venting not only usually doesn't work, but it often is counter-productive because it increases or at least perpetuates the emotion. It typically not only fails to solve the problem, but it often makes it worse. If you were to remain emotionally immature and use venting as your preferred tactic, your destiny may be life imprisonment.

You've probably already learned from your own experience that neither ignoring nor venting works well.

What were you taught as a child? Well, if your parents were good ones, you were probably taught to avoid either ignoring or venting. You were probably trained to take a time out, which at least has the virtue of avoiding the two extreme reactions.

If so, that tactic may have persisted into adulthood. Once when I was in his office, I said something to my dissertation director that he really didn't like. He didn't immediately say anything in response, but he swiveled his office chair around and looked out the window at the Iowa River for a minute or two. That was his way of taking a time out. He was annoyed and settled down before resuming our conversation. It's a tactic than can work well for weak emotions.

It's useless, though, for powerful emotions. In fact, by taking a time out you may only increase the power of the emotion by thinking about it. Have you ever, for example, taken anger and thought it into rage?

What's the best tactic that most adults have for dealing with powerful unwanted emotions?

The sublimation myth is the hopeful idea of using a powerful unwanted emotion to create something good from it. It's the tactic of rising above something negative to make something positive. It's rechanneling the energy from an unwanted emotion to do something positive with it.

This is the best tactic that most adults have for dealing with powerful distressing emotions.

You've probably used it. When you last became really upset about something, perhaps you did some strength training, went for a long walk, or washed and waxed your car. You actually succeeded in turning a negative into a positive. That's successful sublimation.

Because of the physical exertion, you may have actually felt better, too. You may have gotten some good work done as well. However, sublimation leaves the underlying emotion untouched. It cannot work for that because it doesn't address the root problem. Sublimation is a noble failure and can never be anything more. As we shall see in Chapter 7, emotions are, in part, bodily. It's not just that a healthy brain is required for flourishing emotionally, but it's also that emotions actually have a bodily location. Eating well, exercising well, and getting sufficient sleep and relaxation can be emotionally helpful. [I discuss this kind of balancing in <u>Introduction to Living Well</u>.] They certainly cannot cause emotional distress.

A final tactic that doesn't work well is one that I myself only learned about as an adult. It had never occurred to me. It's **the myth of the irrationality of emotions.**

This is the simple idea that emotions are always irrational or senseless. Believe it or not, I first learned of this idea from a clinical psychologist. I was struggling emotionally, and I asked for some good reading recommendations on the nature of emotional well-being. I had admitted to myself that I was failing to flourish emotionally and wanted some help. What answer did I receive? I was told that there are no such books because emotions are irrational!

As I explain in Chapter 7, this is simply nonsense. There's no such thing as an irrational emotion. Review your own emotional history. If a loved one died and you felt grief, was that irrational? Certainly not. It was an intelligible reaction to a loss. If someone unexpectedly punched you in the face and you got angry, was that irrational? Certainly not. It was an intelligible reaction to an assault. If you were disgusted when you learned that a mob had lynched someone without a fair hearing, was that irrational? Certainly not. It was an intelligible reaction to an injustice.

There's a rational explanation for our experiencing every emotion. Sometimes, emotions are too weak or too strong. Sometimes, emotions are inappropriate. Nevertheless, they never just happen for no reason whatsoever. Mother Nature gave them to us and they have survived because they are often useful.

Still, they can be puzzling, especially when it comes to treating them. After all, what is emotional well-being? What is emotional wisdom? Many philosophers have considered this question, and many have theorized about it. There is no agreed-upon answer.

Some famous answers strike me as strange. For example, after Plato, Aristotle is almost always ranked as the second greatest fundamental thinker in the western philosophic tradition. He considers wisdom with respect to anger. Of course, we've all experienced anger. That's easy to do. He thinks of wisdom with respect to anger as learning the practical skill of learning how to get angry at "the right person, in the right amount, at the right time, for the right end, and in the right way [which] is no longer easy, nor can everyone do it." [Nicomachean Ethics, 1109a27-8, Irwin, tr.]

What? The idea that there is a right way to get angry is wildly off the mark. Sages who flourish emotionally never get angry. It's incoherent to think that someone could simultaneously be a slave to anger while enjoying emotional well-being, which is liberation from unwanted emotions.

If you are confused about not yet understanding emotional wisdom, you are in excellent company. Don't beat yourself up; instead, realize that, unlike stupidity, the great feature of ignorance is that it's curable.

Let's turn to a consideration of a fruitful way to understand emotions.

7:

The Nature of All Emotions

Every emotion is composed of three nonemotional parts. The first part is a belief about some situation. The second part is a self-interested evaluation of that situation. The third part is a bodily sensation. Let's get clear about each of these in turn.

The **first** part is a belief about some situation, some state of affairs that's taken to be real. A *"thought"* is an understanding or conceptualization of some situation such as "mother just died." A thought that we take to be true or attach to is a *belief* such as the belief that "mother just died." Emotions are never empty; they are always *about* some particular situation (circumstance, fact, event, object, state of affairs) or other. It's possible to be emotional about anything that we notice. In other words, the objects of emotions are just ordinary objects that we understand as usual, that we apprehend using our conceptual filters.

Because thoughts can be mistaken, beliefs, too, can be mistaken. Apprehensions may be indistinguishable from misapprehensions. There may be no phenomenological difference between something real and something unreal. That's why misapprehensions can be as believable as apprehensions. What we judge to be real need not actually be real. There are such phenomena as illusions and delusions. This is a sufficient reason why we should be humble when it comes to attaching to thoughts about reality. Especially with respect to beliefs based on perception or memory, it's wise always to be more skeptical than fanatical. Philosophers have been arguing for that for literally thousands of years.

A belief doesn't have to be true to be the core (essence, center, heart) of an emotion. However, there cannot be an emotion without a (true or false) belief at its core. In other words, although the situations that we become emotional about do not have to be real, they have to be taken to be real. Unless you believe that your mother just died, you won't experience any emotions about it.

Furthermore, even beliefs that come from veridical perceptions and memories are never the whole truth. Again, that's logically impossible. Again, beliefs are kinds of thoughts. All thoughts are conceptualizations, and all concepts are principles of classification. Therefore, all thoughts are conceptualizations, which means that they can, at best, only be partial. Even true thoughts are only about part of reality. In fact, realizing this is a way of quickly dissolving unwanted emotions [This is the method advocated by Byron Katie I refer to in Chapter 8].

Notice that it's possible to become emotional about what is unreal. This can happen, for example, in nightmares or mental illness. In other words, the belief that is the core of an emotion need not even be partially true.

It can be helpful to notice that moods are generalized emotions; in other words, unlike emotions they need not be about particular situations. Moods and emotions are not clearly divisible. This is actually important in the sense that the tactics that work for dissolving unwanted emotions also work for dissolving unwanted moods such as melancholy or euphoria.

The **second** part of an emotion builds upon its first part, namely, the apprehension of the situation that is real or taken to be real. Let's use a concrete example to focus attention on it. Let's suppose that you are not now located in Kyoto and also that you don't know anyone there or have any business there. Let's also suppose that it's snowing now in Kyoto. How do you feel about that? What emotion are you experiencing?

You aren't experiencing any emotion about that, are you? Why would you? It's irrelevant to you. Let's turn this around and admit that *we are never emotional about situations that are or seem to be irrelevant to our lives.*

There are only two ways that situations are relevant to us: they either relate to us positively or negatively. If they are neutral to us, then they are not relevant to us. This is why there's an evaluation at the core of every emotion. The initial evaluation typically happens so quickly that we may not even realize it, which is why it would not be unreasonable to combine the first two parts of an emotion into one by claiming that emotions are **evaluative apprehensions**.

The core of every positive emotion is "*this is good for me*" and the core of every negative emotion is "*this is bad for me.*" These are evaluative, not descriptive, judgments. Descriptive judgments are not emotions; they are just thoughts. Descriptive beliefs are also not emotions; they are just thoughts that we think are true. Emotions always have an evaluative judgment at their core.

In this sense, all emotions are self-involved. The evaluative judgments at their core are egocentric. It need not be the case that a situation really is good or bad *for me* in order for me to be emotional about it, but there must be a *for me* or there wouldn't be an emotion.

Now that it's been pointed out, it may seem obvious to you. However, if it doesn't seem obvious, please try to think of a counterexample from your own experience. For example, recall a situation that enraged you without the presumption that it was bad for you in some way. In other words, emotions are not about reality. Emotions are about our surrealities, our individual experiences of reality. Your emotions are not about *the* world; your emotions are about *your* world. The **third** part of an emotion can actually seem to be missing when emotions are very weak. There can be borderline cases in which we are not sure whether or not to think of a feeling as an emotion. Still, without a clear distinction or difference between paradigmatic examples, there could not be any borderline cases. In other words, borderline cases presuppose a concept; they don't undermine it.

The final part of an emotion is that it is bodily. It's a bodily feeling or set of feelings; it's a physiological sensation or set of sensations. When we notice that our welfare is on the line, we feel it or experience it physiologically.

Different people experience emotional sensations in different ways. They may experience them in different parts of the body. For example, I may experience anger in my throat, and you may experience it in your gut. We may experience similar situations with different emotional intensities.

Notice that different emotions are often accompanied by different desires. If you are angry at someone, you want to punish that person. If you are sad about a loss, you want to regain it. And so on.

We often differ, though, in how quickly we notice emotional sensations as well as how quickly they dissipate. Even though our emotional make-ups differ and the qualities of our emotional sensations differ, without any bodily sensation or noticeable physiological feeling at all, there's simply no emotion.

Of course, many bodily sensations or feelings have nothing to do with emotions or beliefs at all. It's only when they are intimately connected to evaluative apprehensions that bodily sensations are parts of emotions.

This threefold analysis of emotions is not original. I didn't think of it. Many philosophers accept it. I know of no good objection to it. You'd be foolish, though, not to examine it for yourself. Test it against your own emotional experiences. You don't experience emotions in others; you experience them directly. You're the expert on your own emotions. Pay attention to them and determine for yourself whether or not emotions always have these three parts. If you have not done that for yourself yet, please stop reading and do it.

Please don't just recall some powerful unwanted emotions you've experienced and subject them to this analysis. Also ask yourself: given this analysis, how might it be possible to kill unwanted emotions? After all, emotions themselves can kill us. However, if we kill them first, they won't. In other words, given this analysis, is there a way to emotional peacefulness? Is there a way either to prevent unwanted emotions from arising in the first place or to eliminate them quickly (along with their deleterious effects) after they've arisen? Please wonder about that before reading the next chapter.

8:

How to Kill an Unwanted Emotion Reactively

The "promoting peacefulness" method (technique, tactic) is the method that I recommend for most people. This, too, is not original with me. I initially learned it from Christen Mickelsen who has said he learned it from David R. Hawkins, M.D., Ph.D. [See, for example, Hawkins's Transcending The Levels of Consciousness, pp. 100-101.] Sages such as Eckhart Tolle and Thich Nhat Hanh have also made similar recommendations.

Essentially, like love and joy, peacefulness is a characteristic of our personal cores. You need not try to force yourself to believe that. Instead, experience it yourself. The way to do that is simply to dissolve obstructions to peacefulness, which is what this method does. The promoting peacefulness method has five steps.

First, just *decide* to do something about emotional distress. Just doing that is accepting responsibility for your emotional health, taking charge of the quality of your emotional life. Assuming that you're not already a sage, without that degree of maturity, you'll remain a prisoner to all the unwanted emotions you experience. You'll remain as out of control emotionally as children. As you'll confirm when you do it, it's much, much better to take charge and gain control of emotions to free yourself from emotional bondage rather than remaining stuck there.

Especially if you have never before realized that it's possible never to suffer from prolonged emotional distress, this commitment to yourself is the most important step. With it and persistence, you will succeed by mastering this or some similar method (and I suggest another one below as well).

Second, *single out* (identify, pick out) the unwanted emotion that is obstructing emotional peacefulness. How? Think of the situation, which you judge bad for you, that's giving rise to your being emotionally upset or distressed. As you remind yourself of it and make the uncomfortable and counterintuitive decision to pay attention to it instead of trying to distract yourself from it, *notice where in your body you are feeling it.* Try to pinpoint its location exactly. Please don't be satisfied with just selecting a general area such as your throat or stomach, try to *focus precisely* on the center of the sensation, in other words, on the point at which it's most intense. If it's possible, it may help to put the tip of your forefinger over it. Just notice it – and, if necessary keep noticing it. It may move and shift locations. If it does, just stay with it. It may become stronger or weaker. Just keep focusing on it.

Third, *accept* it unconditionally. Surrender to it completely. Let it hurt! It won't kill you. In effect, this is loving it, accepting it just as it is. This step, too, seems counterproductive. You may be in the bad habit of distracting yourself from feeling unwanted emotions. That's a terrible habit. Why? An unwanted emotion is part of your life. If you fail to accept it, you're fighting with yourself, which always results in your being a guaranteed loser.

Think of that unwanted emotion as like a crying baby. What does the baby want? Attention. When we hold and rock and soothe a crying baby, it almost always stops crying. Would it be better, say, to lock the crying baby in a closet in the basement so you don't hear its cries? Certainly not.

Of course, that's just an analogy. In the case of unwanted emotions, if you follow this peacefulness process method, it will always work. Please don't distract yourself either! Just keep accepting it. Just keep giving it your complete attention and loving acceptance. It's that simple.

Fourth, keep attending to it for as long as it takes; just *be* with it. Just continue the third step for as long as required.

Often, the sensation will disappear in less than 5 minutes! Sometimes, it may take several sessions over the course of a few days or, occasionally, some weeks or months. It doesn't matter. Just attend to it as long as you are able to feel it at all.

There's no correlation between the intensity of the sensation or importance of an emotion and how long this process takes. Sometimes, an important emotion that you've been suffering from for years may dissolve in a few minutes. Sometimes, a rather unimportant emotion may take several sessions over a few weeks. There's nothing to think about. There are no judgments to make. Just keep noticing it. This brings us to the critical mistake that, if you make it, will undermine the success of this peacefulness process method.

Do not try to make the unwanted emotion go away. Why? Resisting it will only perpetuate it. *Thinking is resisting*, so just the thought "I want to be free from this emotion" is resisting it. Don't fight feeling it in any way. The key is unconditional positive regard. Surrender to it completely. Love it until it disappears naturally. Accept it until it dissolves completely.

The **fifth** and final step is to ensure that it has completely dissolved. Don't be satisfied with just reducing its intensity. Don't be satisfied with reducing it, say, 95% of the way. Stay with this promoting peacefulness process until the unwanted emotion has completely vanished. To check to ensure that it has 100% disappeared, think again in detail about the initial situation that gave rise to the emotion.

(Mickelsen calls this poking the bear.) Does it bother you *at all*? If so, you have more work to do; keep using this promoting peacefulness process to work on that emotion. If it really doesn't bother you at all, it really has disappeared completely. Furthermore, it'll never come back.

Sometimes unwanted emotions come in layers and it's important to continue working through all of them.

Again, typically, one unwanted emotion leads to an additional unwanted emotion. When that happens, it can be difficult to single out just one to work on. Do your best. Start with the most obvious one and work on that. When it has dissolved completely, just think again in detail about the initial situation to determine if it has any other unwanted emotions associated with it. If it does, single one out to work on. Be patient. Just keep doing this until they have all dissolved. After all, you're just being patient with yourself. Give yourself a break.

Notice that this method does not require any deep background analysis of the situation that gave rise to the emotion in the first place. Emotional well-being or health does not require, for example, years of counseling, psychoanalysis, or psychotherapy.

Peacefulness is a neutral feeling. There's simply no sensation left. If you happen instead to feel a positive emotion such as happiness, that's fine, but it's unnecessary. As long as no unwanted emotion associated with the initial situation remains, your work of freeing yourself is done. Good for you!

If for some reason you want a different reactive method, I've written in <u>Emotional Facelift</u> about the "emotional humility" method popularized by Bryon Katie. There's also a video I did on it, namely, video #15 in the Emotional Empowerment playlist on my DENNIS BRADFORD PHD YouTube Channel. You may also learn it from her books. It's a more intellectual reactive method and, so, may appeal to some people more than this promoting peacefulness method. In my experience, though, the promoting peacefulness method is the best method ever devised for most people for dissolving unwanted emotions as quickly and easily as possible.

Mastering either method yields the same freedom from unwanted emotions. Just the fact that there are two different methods that work may increase your belief that freedom from emotional bondage really is possible.

That's all there is to it! *Master one method and for the rest of your life you'll have an effective technique for freeing yourself from any unwanted emotion.* You'll have mastered an important skill that will serve you well indefinitely. There'll be no need to master any additional method. You'll have learned how to take charge of your emotions. You'll have mastered them. You'll have become wise with respect to emotions and may enjoy emotional well-being for the rest of your life.

9:

Another Way to Obstruct Emotions Proactively

Chapter 3 contains instructions for mastering one classic, effective meditative practice, namely, aliveness awareness. If you don't already have a daily spiritual practice and are not now doing aliveness awareness daily, reading that chapter was a useless waste of time for you.

Benefitting from practicing requires practicing, not thinking about practicing. If you are stuck reading and learning about how to improve the quality of your life, you are stuck. To get unstuck and feel and be and do better, begin practicing daily. If that applies to you, take it as tough love.

One of the problems that we all have is that we get stuck thinking negatively. Why?

Here's one way to think of it: do you spend more time thinking about solved problems or about unsolved problems? Surely the answer is the latter. What's to think about with respect to solved problems? Just learn any lesson about what happened and move on.

It's different with respect to all unsolved problems. Since they are not yet solved, we may worry that, not only haven't we solved them already, but also we may never solve them. Even if we understand how to solve them, we may be blocked by various situations from solving them. Even if we understand how to solve them and are not blocked from solving them, we may worry about which one it would be best to solve first. We may also worry about the possible consequences of solving them. In other words, there always seems to be a lot to worry about!

You've probably known people who relish and collect grievances. They are poisonous people best avoided. Sometimes, though, it's difficult or impossible to avoid them and their negativity can seem to affect us negatively.

The world is in constant flux. Just because I solve a problem yesterday does not mean that I'll be able to solve it tomorrow. That applies not only to simple problems whose solutions are required to sustain our lives (for example, where is my next meal coming from?) but also to other-directed problems (for example, how can I help feed others?) It's easy to have unsolved problems as a kind of constant companion.

There's nothing abnormal about that. You are not mentally ill or unstable if the negative seems often to outweigh the positive. It would be good, though, to have a daily corrective that at least balances the negative with something more positive.

That's the goal of **gratitude journaling**.

Let's suppose that you already are doing a daily meditative practice such as aliveness awareness [Chapter 3] and also that you are doing morning pages [Chapter 4]. I hope that you are. Both are excellent practices. Any classic meditative practice will help undermine unwanted emotions before they have a chance to infect you and morning pages is an effective way of doing a brain drain to flush unwanted, undesirable, or negative thoughts from your mind at the beginning of every day.

Gratitude journaling is a way of emphasizing what's positive. It's an extremely helpful corrective to what's negative by rebalancing. It's simple to do. Here's how.

After you write at least 3 morning pages, take a bit more time and handwrite a list of whatever you're grateful for. That's it! Whereas morning pages has a minimum length, gratitude journaling doesn't. Some mornings you'll not write a long list and other mornings you may write a long list. Some mornings you may not write anything at all. What gratitude journaling does is to rebalance your thoughts by strengthening those that are positive. Without it, or some similar practice, it's too easy to become absorbed by negative thoughts.

Record what you appreciate and are thankful for. You may think of daily gratitude journaling as a daily thanksgiving prayer (except that you are not praying to some personal god). You may include why you are grateful for certain things. You may talk about how you do, or should, express gratitude towards others.

Feel free to go online and research tips on how best to do gratitude journaling. If, for example, you find that doing it three times weekly is more effective for you than doing it daily (as some people find), then do it three times weekly rather than daily.

It's not important to spend much clock time doing it. 2 minutes daily or 5 minutes daily is fine. Do more whenever you feel like it. The key is to *do it regularly* even if not daily. Since you are, or should be, doing morning pages daily, it won't be difficult to do it initially every day. *Test* it for 90 days. If at the end of 90 days, you feel that it's working well for you, as I predict you will, keep doing it indefinitely. If you don't feel that it's doing anything to undermine negativity, then just concentrate on your spiritual practice such as aliveness awareness and morning pages. Of the three kinds of practices discussed in this book, the most important is your classic spiritual practice, whether that's aliveness awareness, zazen, or some other classic practice. In addition, doing a brain drain with morning pages will certainly unleash your creativity and doing a gratitude journal will compensate for your natural tendency to think negative thoughts.

You're training yourself to use rather than to misuse thoughts. Furthermore, you now have the peacefulness process to dissolve any negative emotions that arise anyway.

If you've not been using anything similar previously, by using these simple practices, you'll be gifting yourself and those around you with value that's worth more than thousands of times the price you paid for this book.

There's one serious objection, though, that may be blocking your evolution. Let's consider it in the next chapter.

10:

Objection and Reply

The practices promoted in this book work. They are not, though, the only practices that work. Therefore, if you want the benefits that come from any of these practices and yet they don't seem to work well for you after an honest trial, find a replacement practice and test it.

Are you really happy? If not and you'd like to be, since happiness is your birthright as a human being, your task is to find out what you need to do to become happy and do it. Plenty of help is available [See Suggestions for Further Reading and the Appendix below].

You may have lots of objections to the ideas promoted in this book in support of the recommended practices. All or nearly all of them will be dissolved simply by mastering the recommended practices. The danger is that the theorizing is endless, which opens the possibility that you may get stuck theorizing and not ever become significantly happier.

There is one objection or worry, though, that's important to answer initially. I've had otherwise successful people ask me about it. It's this:

What if these practices work? What if I master them and they are actually successful in doing what you claim? What if I empower myself emotionally and kill emotions? Won't I then become emotionally dead like a zombie? Won't I, for example, lose the ability to love?

If you thought you'd lose the ability to love, then this objection would justifiably stop you from practicing and, so, stop you from obtaining the benefits that arise from practicing. The correct response to this version of the objection is this: instead of obstructing your ability to love, killing emotions essentially enhances your ability to love.

What is love? The noun 'love' comes from the verb '(to) love.' What is it to love? It's to act in such a way that benefits the beloved. Loving is giving. Instead of receiving something, it's giving something. Therefore, the more self-centered we are, the more our ability to love is inhibited, and the less self-centered we are, the more our ability to love is enhanced.

Remember from Chapter 7 that all emotions at their core are self-centered. It's because they are self-centered that what often passes for love really isn't love at all. For example, if you get married to enhance your sex life or to diminish your loneliness or to achieve greater social status, you're not acting in a loving way; instead, you're just trying to use someone else for your own purpose(s).

This is why sages are the greatest lovers. Sages are the least self-centered people. They are other-directed and primarily concerned with the welfare of those they love rather than with using their beloved to enhance their own lives. They lead lives of selfless service.

The more you kill emotions, the more sage-like you'll become.

Imagine a child having a temper tantrum. Is that child free to act otherwise? No. That child is living in emotional slavery. Do sages have temper tantrums? Of course not. Children are not free to love. The emotionally immature are not free to love. People with low self-esteem are not free to love. Sages are free to love. Sages live in emotional freedom. Sages have so worked on themselves and transcended their egocentricity that they have become the most loving people there are. It's as if their attachment to themselves has so diminished that their need for self-esteem has dissolved. Their personal selves have dissolved into the Self.

As long as your brain is healthy, you'll automatically keep having thoughts. Furthermore, you'll keep having emotions. That's life. The problem arises only with unwanted emotions, those that cause distress and persist.

What if the practices promoted here work? You'll simply never have to endure prolonged emotional distress. It's in that sense that you'll become free from emotional bondage and more loving, more creative, and more grateful. That's what's ahead for you for the rest of your life if you master the practices recommended in this book (or similar ones that do the same thing).

Furthermore, you'll also automatically be setting a better example of emotional well-being for those around you.

11:

Bonus

There's an automatic additional bonus as well.

Ask yourself, "Am I attracted to people who love me? Do I enjoy being around loving people? Do I naturally value those who give to me (as opposed to those who try to use me or take from me)? Am I attracted more to happy people than to unhappy people?" We all are. Life is difficult enough as it is without surrounding ourselves with hateful takers who are unhappy.

The additional bonus is that *the more like sages we become, the more others will find us attractive and want to be in our presence.* For social animals like us, this is not an insignificant bonus. If you want more friends or lovers, stop worrying about theoretical objections to the practices recommended here and instead get practicing to master them. The only obstacle to becoming more loving is you. The only obstacle to becoming more attractive to others is you.

The real cure for our interpersonal ills is for everyone to become a philosopher ever ready to question all thoughts. The three methods promoted in this book are ways of living an examined life. Everyone can do all three. They are practical aids to living well, which means living a life of nonattachment. That's freedom from conceptual and emotional bondage and freedom for love.

I hope that you've found reading this book really beneficial. If so and you know someone else who might benefit from reading it, please recommend it to that person. That would be an act of love.

I thank you for your attention and wish you all the best.   9 Jan 21

Dennis E. Bradford

About the Author

Dennis E. Bradford is a philosopher who holds a diploma from Blair Academy, a B.A. from Syracuse University, an M.A. from The University of Iowa, and a Ph.D. from The University of Iowa. Panayot Butchvarov, Distinguished Professor Emeritus of Philosophy at The University of Iowa, was his dissertation director.

Dr. Bradford has been a philosopher since 1964. He taught philosophy and humanities at SUNY Geneseo for 32 years. He taught all the major philosophers from both the western and the eastern philosophical traditions and routinely counseled students.

Christian Mickelsen was his coaching mentor. Dr. Bradford not only holds certification as a qualified personal coach from the Rapid Results Coaching Academy but also he's undergone Instant Miracle Mastery training and been certified as an Instant Miracle Master.

He's a former member of MENSA and the American Philosophical Association.

He's the author of over 30 books and has been an Amazon Bestselling Author. To view his Amazon Author

Central page, go to this link: 'https://www.amazon. com/s?i=digitaltext&rh=p_27%3ADennis+E.+Brad- ford&s=relevancerank&text=Dennis+E.+Brad- ford&ref=dp_byline_sr_ebooks_1 He's also published numerous articles, including 20 at https://ezinearticles. com/, and well as several hundred blog posts at den- nis-bradford.com. He has multiple websites including consultingphilosopher.com and endfearfast.com.

He's been a member of the Rochester Zen Center and became a formal student of The Venerable Bodhin Kjolhede, Roshi, in 2000. Dr. Bradford has had a daily meditation practice since 1994. He volunteered leading meditation groups at different prisons for many years.

He spent 2 years as a lieutenant in the U.S. Army with overseas duty in Korea before attending graduate school.

He played (full-contact) hockey for many years in the Rochester Metro Hockey league.

He lives peacefully in his home on the shore of Conesus Lake in upstate New York.

Suggestions for Further Reading

How to Dissolve Unwanted Emotions

A Course in Miracles

The Power of Now

A New Earth

The Three Pillars of Zen

Loving What Is

The Fundamental Wisdom of the Middle Way

Waking from Sleep

Basic Teachings of the Buddha

In the Buddha's Words

The Upanishads

Appendix:

Getting More Help

Are you familiar with the Hawthorne effect? It's a psychological effect that comes from psychological stimulus/response studies. How do we react when we realize that we're being observed? It turns out that we will typically modify our behaviors in response to becoming aware that someone is watching us. Businesses and other organizations such as governmental agencies make use of it frequently. Over time the power of the Hawthorne effect wears off, but nevertheless it can be quite useful.

For example, suppose that you've never had a meditative practice before and decide to test aliveness awareness for yourself. One way to enhance your experience is simply to imagine that I am somehow watching you every day for the first month as you practice. If you do that, it may well stimulate you to practice more perfectly even though in this case the observer is imaginary.

Interestingly, our brains cannot easily tell the difference between what is real and what isn't. Reality is not a phenomenal quality such as being red or being circular. To be real is to be multiply singleoutable, usually the subject of multiple identity judgements [For more on this, see my The Concept of Existence or Butchvarov's Being Qua Being.] This is why we can be fooled into having emotional reactions to what isn't real in dreams or mental illness. It's also why just imagining someone watching you can stimulate you to improve your behavior.

Still, after a month, the power of the Hawthorn effect may diminish. You may also want to add, say, a walking program into your daily routine. If you do, imagine your exercise coach watching you as you walk. Even better, hire a coach to watch you! So many people are doing that that the online coaching industry right now is booming. Do you want to attract a mate? Do you want to become a better lover? Do you want to dissolve unwanted emotions that persist? Do you want to lose body fat? Do you want to launch your own business? Do you have a serious problem with a child you want to work through successfully? Hire a coach!

Because of the Hawthorne effect, simply hiring someone to watch you may by itself stimulate you to modify your behavior. Of course, it's best to hire a coach who has expertise in whatever you are trying to do and with whom you quickly develop rapport. A good coach will not only "hold space" for you to develop but will also help guide your development.

Suppose that you want more peace of mind and more emotional empowerment. What's the most important criterion you should look for with respect to hiring a coach? Although the value of hiring a coach is relatively well-known, the answer to that critical question is not relatively well-known.

The most important criterion is the coach's degree of happiness. It's true that that's not really measurable, but, fortunately, our degree of reported happiness correlates directly with what can be measured, namely, our level of consciousness or degree of wakefulness. This has been known for a long time. For example, the Buddha distinguished four different levels of awakening.

The more conscious (awake, attentive, aware) someone is, the happier that person is and the more loving that person is. Someone's personal "awakeness" or energy level can be measured (calibrated, detected) by using muscle testing. [For more on this, see the books of David R. Hawkins, M.D., Ph.D., such as <u>Power Vs. Force</u>, <u>The Eye of the I</u>, and <u>I</u>.]

So, if you are even thinking about hiring a coach, I recommend that you look not just at that coach's credentials or expertise in the area that interests you most but also at that coach's ability to love you, to support and encourage you to do what's best for you (in exchange, of course, for the money you invest in the coaching). Coaching is a collaboration, an exchange of value.

How, though, is it possible for anyone who is not an expert to recognize someone who is an expert? If you yourself are an expert, you don't need to hire an expert to help you help yourself. However, if you yourself are not an expert, you are liable to be conned.

This is a general problem concerning hiring anyone from a plumber to a personal coach. Assuming that you're not (yet!) a sage, how is it possible for you to recognize a sage who would be a loving coach? It's not. Sadly, there is no standard certification and there are con artists in every field.

If your personal goal is to become a sage, the good news that it is not initially necessary to find a sage to help you. However invaluable it might be, the personal help of a sage is not necessary in the beginning. (All the sages I've personally known began their quests by reading books or taking courses.)

Instead, all that you need to do is to find someone who has successfully solved your problem to help you to solve it, too. If that person has a track record of helping others do the same thing, so much the better.

Once you understand that your personal consciousness calibration correlates with your degree of happiness, it becomes obvious that the way to become happier is to increase your personal calibration. Although it's typically difficult to find a sage to help you one-on-one, it is much easier to find a personal coach to help you one-on-one. If you want that kind of help, the key is to find a coach who has a sufficiently high personal calibration.

If you'd like to hire one and have some money to invest, the good news is that there are such coaches available to help you. How might you recognize one?

My recommendation is that you contact some to see if they'll buy you an initial coaching session. Start by doing browser searches or by looking at relevant groups in social media platforms. It not only is possible to do this without spending any money, but also if a coach agrees to buy you an initial session you'll be able at least to determine for yourself the initial degree of rapport between the two of you. If someone is a con artist in a field in which you're not an expert, that person will more easily be able to con you on the level of thoughts than on the level of emotions. That's why it's wise simply to have a conversation with that person and "listen" to your gut.

If your own personal calibration is sufficiently high and you happen to know muscle testing, you could also or alternatively test that prospective coach's calibration yourself. The higher your own personal calibration and the better you are at muscle testing, the more accurate that calibration is likely to be.

Unfortunately, if you happen to have a low personal calibration or have little or no experience muscle testing, you won't be able to do that. You may, though, be able to find or perhaps hire someone else who is qualified to calibrate a prospective coach for you. [If you are stuck and would like to hire me for a modest, one-time fee to calibrate one or several prospective coaches for you, simply email me at <u>dennis@endfearfast.com</u> and tell me what you'd like to do. If I happen to know a prospective coach's calibration already, I'll give it to you free. At the time of this writing, the only life coaches I know who have sufficiently high personal calibrations are me and Christian Mickelsen, but there are many other coaches I've not calibrated for myself. Mickelsen is extremely expensive; currently it'd cost you six figures just for one day of coaching.]

If you're not acutely suffering emotionally, it's usually a good idea to straighten out your thinking by reading books and taking courses by those who have mastered the art of thinking. As an undergraduate I read some relevant books such as Philip Kapleau's <u>The Three Pillars of Zen</u> and Alan Watts's <u>This is It</u>. Although I found their ideas interesting, I never made use of them until I experienced an emotional crisis later in life. [To forestall similar reactions, in <u>How To Dissolve Unwanted Emotions</u>, I explain in detail how to use the information from Chapter 8 to benefit yourself and others.]

Another frequently beneficial procedure that may not cost you a penny is to find a qualified spiritual teacher who regularly teaches groups and become a member of that group.

Still, *if you want fast results* find a personal coach with whom you are quickly able to establish a connection that feels right to you. If you happen to like that idea, let me offer an even more specific suggestion. Assuming I'm still doing them when you read this, because you've invested your time and money in this book and are still interested, *I'm willing to buy you an initial emotional assessment coaching session* with me to help you. It will include at no charge my own calibration of your current level of consciousness.

I spent 32 years full-time as a professor teaching philosophy in the classroom. I've authored dozens of books and several have been on emotional empowerment. I'm a certified life coach as well as a certified Instant Miracle Master. I'm a former member of MENSA and have studied and taught all the major philosophers from both the western and eastern philosophic traditions. In short, I certainly have the required background.

So, if you're interested in living better emotionally, using the Hawthorne effect well to your advantage, and in getting more guidance as well as personal support from me, I encourage you to schedule an initial call. There'd be no fee for the call or selling on it.

Why might you find it helpful?

- You'll come away with a crystal-clear vision of what it would be like for you to end emotional confusion and distress and begin flourishing emotionally

- We'll uncover hidden challenges that may be sabotaging either your inner game or your outer game success

- You'll learn your own personal calibration, which will enable you to understand how far your evolution needs to proceed until you experience the next major paradigm shift of consciousness

- You'll leave the session renewed, re-energized, and inspired to do a lot better in terms of your emotional well-being and happiness. How would it work? These sessions typically last between 30 and 90 minutes, but you may want to allow for 2 hours. All that's required is a quiet place to be alone and undisturbed on the phone with me.

Go to: https://calendly.com/dennis-47/session

Just answer the few simple required questions there and select a time that works well for you.

These calls are ends in themselves. The paying clients who invest in my Emotional Empowerment, Living Well, and other coaching packages enable me to be able to afford to give them away.

Our lives are not only terminal but short. By the time you read this, I may not be giving them away anymore. Sorry! (I'm in my mid-70s and may soon retire or die.) If you're interested, therefore, I recommend that you take immediate action and schedule one right now.

If I'm *not* making this offer anymore and you're acutely suffering emotionally, get some help to get you back to normal. Find a suitable consulting philosopher, psychiatrist, clinical psychologist, spiritual teacher, or friend willing and able to help you. If you're enduring normal rather than acute emotional distress, I encourage you to learn more on your own. An excellent start would be to read the books listed on the *Suggestions For Further Reading* above.

Best wishes!